T0290285

me as a dream

POEMS BY ZEVA TYBEL

To my babies,
the most beautiful creations
I could have imagined.

And in memory of Nixon,
my first and biggest baby,
and companion of almost 14 years.

February 20, 2009 - December 27, 2022

May your memory be a blessing.

INTRODUCTION

"He was attracted to my light. I didn't think he would
hate my light because he couldn't have it for himself."
—*Ashley C. Ford on "Unlocking Us," May 19, 2021*

"I thought grief would be like a river,
but in fact, it was an ocean."
—*Saeed Jones on "Death, Sex & Money," October 16, 2019*

"Nobody survives by accident. Survival is a creative act."
—*Ocean Vuong on "We Can Do Hard Things," April 5, 2022*

These three quotes have lived in my head rent-free since the
first time I heard them, spoken by each of these creators as an
off-the-cuff remark on one of the many podcasts I listen to as a way
to fill my days and keep my mind moving. In re-reading the poems
I've composed over the last three years, it became apparent to me
that these themes - abuse, grief, and survival - are core to where
my mindset has been and what my work is about.

The last several years have been tumultuous, to be sure.
In 2018, I was suffering from severe postpartum depression and
anxiety, having given birth to my youngest child in late 2017. My
body kept the score; bones breaking, hernias bulging, gall bladders
failing - I felt like I spent the entirety of that year in the hospital,
recovering from one surgery or another, unable to even lift my baby
while I was still trying to bond with her, begging my spouse for
support, begging the universe for a break, begging my psychiatrist
for medication that would make me feel human again.

As it turns out, my brain, my body – they were not the
problems. The real problem was something far more sinister: The

insecurity that had plagued me from childhood. The self-doubt that had followed me first in my relationship with my parents, then in my relationships with men in my teens and early twenties, and finally into my marriage, where my then-spouse attempted, as all the others did, to assert control and I, being used to forgoing myself in favor of maintaining the peace, did not push back.

This book, these poems, are the pushback. In these pages, you will find all the thoughts I had during the final years of my marriage, during my divorce, and in the years of healing that followed. I am tired of hiding my truth and keeping others' secrets. Grief is an ocean, and I have swum far enough to find an island in this ocean; a tiny sanctuary where I can finally cling to land and the stability it offers.

From here, I will celebrate my survival. From here, I will shine my light.

SHRINK

I walk around bald now
All my hair fell out from the stress
of a decade of being married to you
And so I cut it all off
because I couldn't bear the reminder

I wonder if people look at me
and think
"Is she sick?"
(Isn't that what you asked me
the first time you saw it?)
Or maybe they think
"*Was* she sick?"

The answer is yes.
To all of it.

You ravaged my body like a cancer
and left me for dead
And I lost weight
So much weight
that my family complimented me
on how good I looked
as if how bad I felt
was immaterial

I was shrinking from sadness
the way I shrank in terror around you
Making myself small for fear that
taking up too much space
in my own goddamn home
would invoke your wrath

They had always wanted me to shrink,
and I'd never been able to
But finally I was
And they were happy to see it
And that hurt most of all.

UNDER THE STARS

I started writing again after you left.
What does that say about you?
About who you were to me?
That the only thing I ever truly loved
became something I couldn't do
during the final years of us.

I remember sitting with you once when we were young
under the stars on a hotel balcony,
and thinking about things I wanted
to put down on paper,
and wondering,
how can people not feel this way?
How can people not want to create?

And then you wanted to leave our home behind
So we did
And you wanted to have children
So we did
And over time, I stopped having the drive
I stopped having the energy
to create.
Because I had already created something,
and they are the most beautiful
creations I could have imagined.
and what more could I need?

But I missed it.

And then one day you wanted to leave our life behind
So you did.
And I felt those feelings come back.
Those feelings I had missed for a long time,
because I had already created something beautiful,
and what else did I have to offer?
You made me feel like I had nothing to offer.

But I do.

UNRAVEL

I used to wear your love like a shield
to protect me from the rest of the world

But what I thought was made of steel
impervious to penetration
was loosely woven
and full of holes

Still,
I clung to the thread that held us together
watching it unravel us whole

Lower and lower I go
holding on,
but with every moment
watching us disappear

HINDSIGHT

At some point, there must have been happiness.
At some point, there must have been something beyond
lust and novelty
and the tangible relief of finally
finally
finally
finding someone to make home.

I can still see it sometimes —
the way the ceiling looked in the moonlight
as we laid in bed
our voices rising to the stars
and I could feel myself falling deeper
and wondering how anyone could ever fuck this up

I really thought this was what love was
and that this is how hard it had to be.
That love was work,
your affection payment for services rendered.

I realized before I realized that I realized
that this was not real,
that I deserved more
than happiness as a transaction.

But I soldiered on
in too deep
trapped by my promises
and the security of your love
that I now realize
you had never guaranteed.

There is no going back
or knowing what might have been
if I had trusted myself
instead of trusting you.

SECRETS

It took me years to get to this place
of peace and understanding
of being able to answer for myself
questions that I knew you'd never address

I know exactly who you are now
and I know what kind of man you were
when we were together

I tell you this
not as an accusation
but as a means to lighten my own load
because I am tired of carrying
and keeping
your secrets

THE LEAST-LOVED CHILD

You didn't want to be loved —
you wanted to be worshipped.
Love comes with accountability
and growth
And that was all too much for you to bear,
having to give of yourself
for a greater goal.

In a session with my therapist,
I told her that your parents moved away
Away from you, and all your self-loathing
Away from our heathen children

And I realized for the first time in a long time
that you had never really been joking
about being the least-loved child.
That you had been chasing something with me
that you couldn't find with your parents
Something that you hated them for
and you would eventually hate me for
because I couldn't heal you;
no one can —
you have to do that yourself.

And after years of anger and frustration
I finally felt it —
I felt sorry for you.
Because you are just a child who can't grow up
(or won't, I'm not sure which)
And I tried so hard,
worked so hard,
pleaded with you,
I told you so

But the lesson you finally taught me
is that you can't make people be human.

WHOLE

Married almost fifty years.
The love between you is what I tried to emulate,
only to find that it wasn't love at all
but rather a bond created
by time and trauma.

I fought my way into this experience,
trying to create love with someone
who never even knew what love was
and trying to create a bond with someone
who never even wanted me.

On the other side now, I realize,
these bonds also require the most fundamental aspects
of human connection —
mutual affection, mutual respect.
I'm not sure yours has either.
I know mine didn't.

So I am fighting my way into a new experience now.
One where I first have affection and respect
for myself.
Because my relationship with her
is the most important relationship
I will ever have.

And all the men may come and go
while I treat myself
the way they should have treated me
and model for my girls
what it looks like
to be whole
on my own.

THE ASK

what do you say when they ask
when are you coming home?
or is that a question you even hear?
do they talk to you, wondering aloud,
their fears and hopes swirling around them
like angry ghosts anxious for acknowledgement

you're in our space, they howl,
voices rising above the din of my own endless thoughts
and i shudder

we are all already haunted,
but you could never be.

you never believed.

THE RIGHT THING

I don't always know the right thing to say.

Sometimes I think of it,
even years later;
years too late.

These moments never leave me.
They linger the way old memories do,
asking to be changed
or taken back —
mutated into something else entirely.

But I can't change the past,
and then,
I didn't know the future.

TOGETHER ALONE

I spent so much of our time together alone
surrounded by people,
but alone.

What would it take
to get you to look at me
to get you to talk to me
to get you to see me
to get you to understand
that I'm here, missing you
wondering where you've gone
even though you're right here in front of me
and somehow, also,
nowhere in sight.

LISTEN

I promised myself that this time would be different;
that I would listen to what I needed,
instead of worrying about what I wanted.

But this is the first time I have to listen to myself,
and it's strange.

My own voice sounds so unfamiliar
because I am so used to quieting it —
burying it away amidst the shoulds
and moving forward

But sometimes forward is the wrong direction
which is something I only know now,
that forward and onward are not the same.

So I put out the call
Hello? Can you hear me?
What do I do now?

But I can't hear myself
or maybe I do
but I'm not listening.

SURVIVOR

There is a distance
physical, palpable
the air around us howling
freezing
unrelenting
I don't know what this is
even though you tell me all the time.
You make it clear
crystal
But I don't believe you.
I can't
Something inside me is too afraid
of history repeating itself
Would that be the worst thing?
I survived it once
I can do it again
But do I want to be a survivor?
No.
I want to be free.

SOMETIMES SHORT THINGS
ARE PIVOTAL

This is the last goodnight you said
as I choked back a sob
What does it mean to lose you now
and is it the right thing
and how do I know
if I suddenly have more than one small voice
and they are all telling me different things

HUNGER

You used to grab at my body with the hunger
of a man who hadn't seen food in weeks
and found himself suddenly,
inexplicably,
at a decadent buffet
all his favorite items in abundance
and his for the taking
for the low, low price
of *I love you*

He was mistaken
to think that such a small entry fee
would grant him access to everything he ever wanted

The crab legs are not included
nor is the steak tartare.
And the oysters require negotiation,
longing, as one does, for their homes along the coast,
resentful of their inclusion here;

they never consented to this.

GHOST

Do I look like a ghost to you?
Don't mistake me for gone;
I am still very much alive.

SOIL

You moved me once
And again and again
Uprooting me from the gardens
in which I flourished

This is how they do,
it's said.
They separate
and isolate
so that you're forced to rely
on their ground

And when the ground is poisoned
there's nowhere to go
The gardens in which you flourished
are now full
of other flowers

And so you wilt
and long for what might have been
if you had stayed rooted in the soil
in which you knew you belonged.

36

At eighteen
you become an adult
in the eyes of the law
But what did I know at eighteen?
I was ready to rush into life
with the same defiance and naivete
that I now see in my six-year-old's eyes

And oh, the mistakes
as I ran headfirst into life
desperate for the promises made to me
The rewards for doing *all the right things.*

But *all the right things*
were the wrong things for me
And now here I am,
having completed my first attempt at being grown
and ready to move into the next.

I know better now, I think,
than I did an adulthood ago.
May this second try be the one
where I give myself all the freedom and dignity
that my naive and defiant self wanted
but didn't know how to create
all those years ago.

SOMETHING MORE

Do you ever think about trying again?
Now that we're more than a decade older,
and infinitely wiser
Do you ever think about seeing if
we could overcome the invisible barriers
that kept us distant and dreaming
of something more

I am finally willing to concede
maybe you were something more
all along.

ANEW

Do you know anyone who
after a shipwreck
adrift in their grief
floating aimlessly to land
surviving on hope that tomorrow,
Tomorrow will be the day their feet touch the ground.
Do you know anyone who became someone else?
But also stayed themselves
reaching back into their memory
scraping forth identity
like it was something to be claimed
although it was never truly lost to begin with.
Do you know anyone who started anew
(and is that even possible?)
fresh to "strangers" they'd known all their life
known but unknown to their dearest friends,
a surprise shrouded in familiarity.

HOLDING ON

I worry about you
because I know you can't love yourself
if you fell in love with him
I tried to warn you
but you didn't hear
You didn't want to hear
You wanted to believe that you
and you alone
would make the difference
I don't know how to tell you that he is made of stone
like the men who gazed upon Medusa
And you can climb
but you will never summit
There is no peak
only treacherous cliffs
You can cling
fingertips bloody
your body flailing in the winds
slapping against the jagged rocks
I hope you fall
not because I wish you harm
but because I know
it's the holding on that will kill you.

YOM KIPPUR, 5781

Don't eat, they say, on this Day of Atonement,
the worst thing that you could say to a person
from a culture so obsessed with food
that each of our innumerable holidays
has its own signature meal

Don't eat, they say,
so that you yourself can feel all the weight
of the pain you have caused this year.

And I wonder,
is this even necessary?
In this year where I have felt all the
weight of everyone's pain,
that which I've caused
and that which people have caused me
and that which people have caused
others completely unrelated

In a year that has already taken so much,
that has felt like a never-ending onslaught of
consequences for humans' everyday bad behavior,
what does a Day of Atonement look like?

I want to be inscribed in the Book of
Life, but who is doing the writing?

(Is it God? Because I'd like to have a word with them.)

What are my obligations as someone
who inherited these rites,
who partakes voluntarily of annual self-flagellation
in the journey to being Whole?

What does it mean to feel the weight, one day a year,
when I feel the weight all day every
day of my decisions and,
it seems,
everyone else's?

Don't eat, they say,
but the weight of this world's misery
has made me lose my appetite.

HOMELAND

This homeland was chosen for me
one country abandoned for another
by men and women who never imagined
I'd exist

And here I am
trapped
as the homeland crumbles around me
wondering if it's time to go
the way they must have wondered
as they watched their homelands crumble around them

History repeats itself
again and again
But I've been taught not to trust myself
I've been taught to seek the definite,
not the intuitive

So ancestors, tell me
What do I do?
I am at your mercy
I am full of fear
And I just need to know
How did you know?

RUSTIC CHARM

You can feel the anger rising
but you suck it down
like the brown liquor he loved
that had too much of a bite to it
to quench your thirst
and dull your senses.

Where are the lines between
what is acceptable
and what is not?
Your own model of how to be
a ghost in exile
banished from any homeland
that would have her
(Not that she would have them;
she's quite particular.)

Pray each day
that what's good is also sticky;
Sap stains on a picnic blanket
but instead of ruined,
make it rustic charm.

PIECES

Did I say too much
when you asked me
why we don't have the same name?

I couldn't lie to you
I couldn't betray your trust
the way he betrayed mine.

And so I was honest.
I said that giving up your name
is like giving up a piece of yourself
and that I didn't want to give up any pieces of myself
at all

And especially after he left
the fact that I kept those pieces
felt like a small kindness I had done for myself

I told you I would have been so hurt
to give up those pieces
and still be left behind
(because no amount of pieces I had to offer
were enough for him)

If I was going to be left behind,
I wanted to be my whole self,
the whole time.

UNITED

This country is full of people too
insecure to love themselves
And if they don't even love themselves
how can you expect them to love this country?

VIGILANCE

The sheer exhaustion sets in
after a full day of worry
that we made it to this point
and all that work would be undone
with the launch of a single bullet

I don't like to assume the worst
but we've seen what happens
when we don't prepare for it
when we become complacent
when we believe that the systems
not built for us
will care for us

And so I stayed awake
all night and all day
hoping that my vigilance would keep us safe

I'll never know if it was me
or if it was God,
finally acting,
finally making

OMICRON

Kids who have had COVID are 2.5x more likely to
develop diabetes. Protect yourself and your family
with an N95 mask that is not only cost prohibitive, but
also sold out everywhere. Get tested for COVID, but
half your local testing sites have closed due to staffing
shortages. You can test at home with an antigen test but
they're also cost prohibitive and sold out everywhere.
We're in the midst of a surge of the most contagious
variant of the virus yet. In the background, sirens
blare as democracy crumbles and the planet becomes
increasingly uninhabitable. Enjoy your thirties!

DWELL

It is impossible not to dwell in the past
as I think of all the experiences I've had
and how they could have been different
with a partner who actually loved me

What must it feel like to be supported
or cared for
in the most vulnerable moments of your life?

What must it feel like to be told
What's important to you is important to me
instead of
What's important to you isn't important

I would have been better off alone
with only the thoughts rattling around in my brain
to validate themselves

Because it wasn't these terrible things that broke me;
it was the way you told me they shouldn't even hurt.

THAT PLACE

They came home smelling of that place
and it made me understand
for the first time
why wild animals reject their young
over something as simple
but visceral
as scent

"My other home," she called it
No, I told her
This will always be home
That place is an outpost
on a barren, frozen tundra

You can't make a home
on land that inhospitable

SOMEDAY

Maybe someday
the memory of your betrayals
will be as distant as
the memory of how I ever loved you to begin with

BLOOM

You didn't deserve my forgiveness
but I gave it to you
I wanted so badly to give you everything you needed
Anything to keep you in bloom
But you walked away
uprooted yourself
and let yourself wilt
because you couldn't bear
to have your thirst quenched by my water,
your stalks warmed by my sun

DONE

You were so busy looking
for someone to take care of you,
you didn't even realize
you tried to marry
your mother.

A woman who stays quiet,
compliant.
Shrinks herself
to make you feel big.

That was never going to be me,
and you knew it from the start.
But your hope.
Oh,
the hope.

We were both guilty of it then,
though a part of me
knew better.

That was what shrank
to make the love feel big
to make me feel
like this was right.

But with the love gone,
I'm done shrinking.
For you,
for anyone.

My self is big, and she is bold,
and she will not be told no
by anyone worth having.

ABLAZE

You touch me like a child touches a flame —
an excited curiosity to experience my heat;
sudden fear and regret the moment you feel it.

Where is the person who will see my fire for what it is?
Who won't run away because I burn too hot?

I need someone who wants to be set ablaze.

REASON

What reason do you have not to trust me
beyond the Other Man you invented
to feel morally superior
as you let us crumble
alongside your self-worth

He never existed
and I told you that
and I think you knew
You knew that he was a figment of your imagination
the same imagination that was forever making up facts
and histories
and conversations
that never existed

What reason did I ever give you
to think you weren't the one?
What reason did I ever give you
that wasn't a response to the infinite
reasons you gave me?

Silence
and contempt
and belittlement

But somehow, this is all me
Me and this Other Man

Maybe he does exist,
but he's just the fantasy
of the man you could have been.

HEALTHY

I am basically Jewish, he said,
and I scoffed
mostly at his need to feel persecuted
for his white skin
and the masculinity he cultivated over the years
that left no room for humility
or remorse

This is not a healthy way to be,
always wishing you were someone else
to excuse your insecurities
and devastating mediocrity

He is so quick to say things without meaning them
without even understanding them

Sometimes I wonder what it must be like inside his head
but it's too exhausting

My energy is precious,
and mine alone
and I need it,
not him.

COST

What is the cost
of a love gone wrong?
Lives upended,
and homes and spirits
broken in two.

What is the cost
of staying beyond our time?
Dreams unfulfilled,
and quiet fear
of what destinies
might be lurking on the other side.

To bridge that gap
we paid with our sanity
Exhaustion and melancholy setting in
A cancer upon our bodies and minds

And when it is done
the cost is worth its weight
in freedom
from you and your misery.

FLAMES

You never really knew me
because you never wanted to know.
You envisioned me as a dream,
a fantastical creature you concocted
that needed no more and no less than you

I only wonder now
why your love of independence
and respect for rugged individualism
never seeped into our love

I waited for it,
watching for it,
like smoke under a bedroom door
during a house fire

I shouldn't have had to wait for signs
to confirm what was or wasn't real.
We should have always been in flames.

OUT OF THIN AIR

I created you out of thin air
Imagined what I wanted
and put it out into the universe

"Please, make my dreams come true
I have been waiting for decades
just to be seen"

But what am I imagining
that creates the same person
over
and over
and over

The little things sneak through
The anger and resentment
The reassurance
"It's not about you"
But it could be,
someday

I created you out of thin air
and so you have no people
No roots to hold you firm

Please, these were not the dreams I meant
How much longer will I wait
just to be seen?

STAGNANT

I thought you were stable
but really,
you were stagnant,
afraid to move in space and time,
to explore or push the boundaries
of what could be.

I spent a decade trying to push —
trying to drag you with me
to the places I wanted to go.
I wanted to love you along the way,
but you wouldn't join me.

Is that time wasted?
They say every experience
is an opportunity for growth,
but I'm tired of growing
alone.

STOKED

I feel angry today
the rage is billowing inside of me
like smoke from a fire I didn't know was stoked

There is nervous energy
The tap tap tap of my foot on the floor
A rhythmic backdrop to the eventual explosion
that you never saw coming

Only because you haven't been paying attention.

HURT

What hurt the most
was seeing you be
the person I needed you to be
for everyone but me.

DICHOTOMY

Accusations are confessions
and threats are fears
And so now I know more than I ever wanted to
about what was happening behind the curtain
behind that shroud of silence
that stood where intimacy should be

I am the kind of person who both
wants to know
and also
doesn't want to know
and that dichotomy tears me apart
Because as you once told me
I am the most indecisive person you'd ever met.

What will protect my mind
and what will protect my heart
and is there a solution to protect them both?
Or must I give a part of myself
as a sacrifice
to save another
and to move forward
however slowly

NAPTIME

I want you to sleep.
Feel the nighttime envelop you
in the middle of the afternoon
like an ocean wave lapping at your feet,
the undertow pulling the sand beneath your heels
as it retreats.

It will take you if you let it.

DANCE

She delights in telling me
"Vashti was rude!"
She is so proud she knows this story
passed down from generation to generation
without nuance or shades of gray

Sometimes it's okay to be rude, I tell her
She is quiet, absorbing my words
We all deserve to protect ourselves, I say
To have control over our own bodies
Vashti didn't want to dance.
Why should she dance?

(She doesn't know that "dance"
is a euphemism for something else entirely.)

THE FOG

Now that I'm coming out of the fog
Now that I'm on my tenth (or more) day
of sleeping the world away
like time and obligation is meaningless
to a body that doesn't have the strength
to even make myself a cup of tea
Now that I'm past the worst of it
I realize,
I could have died. I really, really could have.
If it were a year ago,
before the vaccines and the boosters
and the hospitals full to the brim
With people too stupid and selfish
to just follow the goddamn instructions
to wear a mask
and wash your hands
If it were a year ago,
if I didn't have these antibodies in my system
working overtime to help me heal
causing night sweats
(and day sweats if we're being honest)
as my immune system kicks into gear
Kicks into overdrive
Kicks this thing out of my body
so that I can once again be a fully present human
for myself, for my children,
for my friends and family,
for my job that I haven't been to in two weeks

If it were a year ago,
maybe I wouldn't have been able to breathe
and I would have called 911 in desperation
and then my ex in even more desperation
to please come get the kids
because I certainly don't want to
bring them to the hospital
They're too little to be there for that
They're still too small
to be with their mother in her final moments
and to feel that fear
of life as they knew it slipping away from them
The last two years have already taken so much from them
Half of my four-year-old's childhood
Almost all of my seven-year-old's formal schooling
And I want it to be many, many, many years
before they stand by my bedside
and watch me utter my last words
and take my last breath.

YOU

You don't need to try to be them
and you can never be them, anyway.
You are your own;
your very, very own.

JOURNEY

I have been gone for such a long time
I had forgotten how to even be alone
and whole
Shattered into a million pieces by the daily hammering
of life and expectations
of lust and what passed for love

There is still a fire within me
raging as they do now
turning the skies orange
demanding attention
demanding that you step back
and make way
because I am coming through.

And I want to be angry,
(and sometimes I still am,)
but mostly,
mostly I am grateful

You wouldn't set me free
but you let me loose
on this journey
to me.

ACKNOWLEDGEMENTS

First and foremost, to Raeann and Wendy, my sisters, the women who saved my life by supporting me through my darkest days and carrying me when I could not carry myself.

To Jayson, my forever therapist and sounding board, who showed me how to laugh again.

To the friends, family, and strangers who brought this dream to fruition by backing my Kickstarter, including (but not limited to) Dana Hansen, Maurice Matthews, Kaitlin Geballe, Kelly Leaman, Jes Bertrand, Steven and Amy Gottlieb, and Adam Spera.

And to anyone who has ever read or liked anything I've written: Thank you. It is with your support that I even believed I could do this. It is because of you that this book is real.